Advent and Christmas
with
THOMAS MERTON

ADVENT and CHRISTMAS
with
THOMAS MERTON

A Redemptorist Pastoral Publication

Liguori

LIGUORI, MISSOURI

Imprimi Potest:
Richard Thibodeau, C.Ss.R.
Provincial, Denver Province
The Redemptorists

Published by Liguori Publications
Liguori, Missouri
www.liguori.org
www.catholicbooksonline.com

ISBN 0-7648-0843-5

Library of Congress Catalog Card Number: 2002104777

Printed in the United States of America
06 05 04 03   5 4 3

Contents

dvent is a time of waiting, of expectation, of silence. Waiting for our Lord to be born. A pregnant women is so happy, so content. She lives in such a garment of silence, and it is as though she were listening to hear the stir of life within her. One always hears that stirring compared to the rustling of a bird in the hand. But the intentness with which one awaits such stirring is like nothing so much as a blanket of silence.

DOROTHY DAY

Introduction

THOMAS MERTON, O.C.S.O., Trappist monk, hermit, peace activist, poet, retreat leader, and spiritual writer, was one of the most charismatic religious figures of our time. He died in Bangkok, Thailand, in 1968, the result of an accidental shock from an electric fan. He was on a journey to meet with monks of the Eastern spiritual tradition, in which he was greatly interested. His pilgrimage to Thailand, India, and Sri Lanka was his first long journey outside the Abbey of Gethsemani in many years and was part of a search to learn more about those aspects of Asian spiritual traditions that could be applied to Western monasticism. Merton's interest in this area can be seen in his books *Zen and the Birds of Appetite, Mystics and Zen Masters,* and *The Asian Journals of Thomas Merton.*

Born in France in 1915 to an American father and a New Zealand mother, Merton converted to Catholicism in 1938 while he was a student at Columbia University in New York City. This experience is detailed in *The Seven Storey Mountain* (1948), an autobiographical account of his conversion and his eventual decision to enter the Trappist monastery of Our Lady of Gethsemani, located in Kentucky, in 1941. During his initial period at Gethsemani, he wrote *Seeds of Contemplation* and *The Waters of Siloe.*

Merton was ordained a priest in 1949. During the period after ordination, Merton wrote *The Ascent to Truth, Bread in the*

Wilderness, The Sign of Jonas, The Living Bread, No Man Is an Island, and *The Silent Life.* After being appointed Master of the Choir Novices in 1955, Merton penned such books as *New Seeds of Contemplation, The Wisdom of the Desert,* and *Disputed Questions.* It was also during this time that he wrote essays deploring nuclear arms, the war in Vietnam, racial inequality, and violence of all kinds.

Small selections from Father Louis' books (those mentioned in the preceding paragraphs and many more) have been chosen to provide inspiration for the passage through Advent. Even these small paragraphs show Father Louis as a warm and straightforward writer who can speak plainly to his readers. As he wrote in the preface to the Japanese edition of *The Seven Storey Mountain,* "I don't want to speak to you as an author, or a narrator, not even a philosopher, but simply as a friend. I would like to speak to you as your alternate self....If you listen you will hear things that will be said that perhaps are not written in this book. And that will be coming, not from me, but from the One who lives and speaks inside both of us." So, let us begin.

How to Use This Book

ADVENT—that period of great anticipatory joy—is a time of preparation for the celebration of Christ's arrival in Bethlehem as a helpless infant. In the Western liturgy, Advent begins four Sundays prior to December 25—the Sunday closest to November 30 which is the feast of Saint Andrew, one of Jesus' first disciples. The annual commemoration of Christ's birth begins the Christmas cycle of the liturgical year—a cycle which runs from Christmas Eve to the Sunday after the feast of the Epiphany. In keeping with the unfolding of the message of the liturgical year, this book is designed to be used during the entire period from the first Sunday of Advent to the end of the Christmas cycle. The four weeks of Advent are often thought of as symbolizing the four different ways that Christ comes into the world: (1) at his birth as a helpless infant in Bethlehem; (2) at his arrival in the hearts of believers; (3) at his death; and (4) at his arrival on Judgment Day.

Because Christmas falls on a different day of the week each year, the fourth week of Advent is never really finished; it is abruptly, joyously, and solemnly abrogated by the annual coming again of Christ at Christmas. Christ's Second Coming will also one day abruptly interrupt our sojourn here on earth.

Since the calendar dictates the number of days in Advent, this book includes Scripture and meditation readings for a full twenty-eight days. These twenty-eight daily readings make up Part I of this book. It is suggested that the reader begin at the beginning and, on Christmas Day, switch to Part II which contains materials for the twelve days of Christmas. If there are any "extra" entries from Part I, these may be read by doubling up days, if so desired, or by reading two entries on weekends. Alternately, one may just skip those entries that do not fit within the Advent time frame for that particular year.

Part III of this book proposes two optional formats for using each daily entry as part of a longer liturgical observance similar to Night Prayer combined with a version of the Office of Readings. These options are for those who may wish to use this book as part of a more developed individual or group observance. The purpose of these readings is to enrich the Advent/Christmas/ Epiphany season of the liturgical year and set up a means by which individuals, families, or groups may observe the true meaning of the season.

PART I

~~~~~~~~

READINGS *for* ADVENT

DAY 1

[Y]ou know what time it is,
how it is now the moment
for you to wake from sleep.
For salvation is nearer to us now
than when we became believers;
the night is far gone,
the day is near.
Let us then lay aside the works of darkness
and put on the armor of light;
let us live honorable as in the day,
not in reveling and drunkenness,
not in debauchery and licentiousness,
not in quarreling and jealousy.
Instead, put on the Lord Jesus Christ.

ROMANS 13:11–14

Awake, You Sleepers

*M*any of the Zen stories which are almost always incomprehensible in rational terms are simply the ringing of an alarm clock, and the reaction of the sleeper. Usually, the misguided sleeper makes a response which in effect turns off the alarm so that he can go back to sleep. Sometimes he jumps out of bed with a shout of astonishment that it is so late. Sometimes he just sleeps and does not hear the alarm at all....

But we in the West, living in a tradition of stubborn ego-centered practicality and geared entirely for the use and manipulation of everything, always pass from one thing to another, from cause to effect, from the first to the next and to the last and then back to the first. Everything always points to something else, and hence we never stop anywhere because we cannot: as soon as we pause, the escalator reaches the end of the ride and we have to get off and find another one.

ZEN AND THE BIRDS OF APPETITE

✤ ✤ ✤

Lord, be our alarm clock as we make our way through this Advent in expectation of your coming. Keep us from "sleeping at the switch" so that our life of faith has an opportunity to grow and mature in us, and so that our life in the world becomes one of light and honor and love. Above all, let us not sleep through your call. Give us the grace to use this Advent season as a time for our own growth and the growth of our spiritual community. Amen.

❖❖❖❖ DAY 2 ❖❖❖❖❖❖❖❖❖❖❖❖❖❖❖

The steadfast love of the LORD never ceases,
his mercies never come to an end;
they are new every morning;
great is your faithfulness....
The LORD is good to those who wait for him,
to the soul that seeks him.
It is good that one should wait quietly
for the salvation of the LORD....
Although he causes grief, he will have compassion
according to the abundance of his steadfast love;
for he does not willingly afflict
or grieve anyone.

LAMENTATIONS 3:22–26, 32–33

In the Midst of His Love and Mercy

*I*t is only the infinite mercy and love of God that has prevented us from tearing ourselves to pieces and destroying His entire creation long ago....On the contrary, consider how in spite of centuries of sin and greed and lust and cruelty and hatred and avarice and oppression and injustice, spawned and bred by the free wills of men, the human race can still recover, each time, and can still produce men and women who overcome evil with good, hatred with love, greed with charity, lust and cruelty with sanctity. How could all this be possible without the merciful love of God, pouring out His grace upon us?...

THE SEVEN STOREY MOUNTAIN

✣ ✣ ✣

God of light, be the hope of our suffering. Keep us from the darkness of sin and greed; keep us from the mindless quest for superiority and success, from the depravity of hatred and anger. Astonish us with your mercy and love so that we may never forget your faithful compassion. Let us use this time of waiting to recover our bearings and refrain from afflicting anyone with our own sins, no matter how insignificant they may seem to be. Amen.

I wait for the LORD, my soul waits,
and in his word I hope;
my soul waits for the Lord
more than those who watch for the morning.
O Israel, hope in the LORD!
For with the LORD there is steadfast love,
and with him is great power to redeem.
It is he who will redeem Israel
from all its iniquities.

PSALM 130 [129]:5–8

Going Forth to Christ

*A*dvent is the "sacrament" of the PRESENCE of God in His world, in the Mystery of Christ at work in History....

This mystery is the revelation of God Himself in His Incarnate Son. But it is not merely a manifestation of the Divine Perfections, it is the concrete plan of God for the salvation of men and the restoration of the whole world in Christ.

This plan is envisaged not as a future prospect but as a present *fact.* The "last things" are already present and realized in a hidden manner. The Kingdom of God is thus already "in the midst of us." But, the mystery can only be known by those who enter into it, who find their place in the Mystical Christ, and therefore find the mystery of Christ realized and fulfilled *in themselves.*

SEASONS OF CELEBRATION

✤ ✤ ✤

Lord Jesus, assuage our blindness and activate our hearts during this Advent, so that we may find your presence hidden in ourselves. May we unveil the mystery of Christ-with-us and work toward the true restoration of the whole world in your image. Let your light shine in our hearts so that we may always know the truth of your love. Amen.

Arise, shine; for your light has come,
and the glory of the LORD has risen upon you.
For darkness shall cover the earth,
and thick darkness the peoples;
but the LORD will arise upon you,
and his glory will appear over you.
Nations shall come to your light
and kings to the brightness of your dawn....
but the LORD will be your everlasting light,
and your God will be your glory.

ISAIAH 60:1–3, 19

Called Out of Darkness

*E*very baptized Christian is obliged by his baptismal promises to renounce sin and to give himself completely, without compromise, to Christ, in order that he may fulfill his vocation, save his soul, enter into the mystery of God, and there find himself perfectly "in the light of Christ."

As Saint Paul reminds us (1 Corinthians 6:19), we are "not our own." We belong entirely to Christ. His spirit has taken possession of us at baptism. We are the Temples of the Holy Spirit. Our thoughts, our actions, our desires, are by rights more his than our own. But we have to struggle to ensure that God always receives from us what we owe him by right.

LIFE AND HOLINESS

✦ ✦ ✦

O Lord, awake us from the comfortable existence in which we too often may be safely cocooned, and challenge us to accept the call of our baptism. Afflict us with your grace so that we take seriously our efforts to aid the poor, to comfort the sad and lonely, to let our light shine as a beacon to all who may need our help. Allow us to serve also as a wake-up call to our brothers and sisters whose companionship in Christ we share. Amen.

DAY 5

For once you were darkness, but now in the Lord you are light. Live as children of light—for the fruit of the light is found in all that is good and right and true. Try to find out what is pleasing to the Lord. Take no part in the unfruitful works of darkness, but instead expose them. For it is shameful even to mention what such people do secretly; but everything exposed by the light becomes visible, for everything that becomes visible is light.

EPHESIANS 5:8–14

Worthy Beacons

*W*e are supposed to be the light of the world. We are supposed to be a light to ourselves and to others. That may well be what accounts for the fact that the world is in darkness! What then is meant by the light of Christ in our lives? What is "holiness"? What is divine sonship? Are we really seriously supposed to be saints? Can a man even desire such a thing without making a complete fool of himself in the eyes of everyone else...? To tell the truth, many lay people and even a good many religious do not believe, in practice, that sanctity is possible for them. Is this just plain common sense? Is it perhaps humility? Or is it defection, defeatism, and despair?

If we are called by God to holiness of life, and if holiness is beyond our natural power to achieve (which it certainly is) then it follows that God himself must give us the light, the strength, and the courage to fulfill the task.

LIFE AND HOLINESS

✥ ✥ ✥

Christ, Our Redeemer, help us stand firm in the safety of your everlasting light and sustain us in the glorification of your works. Wash us clean with your grace, so that we may be released from our obsession with our own egos and our "own story." Fill our hearts with courage and faith so that we may seriously follow the path to holiness and saintliness. Amen.

DAY 6

[Y]ou say, "I am rich, I have prospered, and I need nothing." You do not realize that you are wretched, pitiable, poor, blind, and naked. Therefore I counsel you to buy from me gold refined by fire so that you may be rich; and white robes to clothe you and to keep the shame of your nakedness from being seen; and salve to anoint your eyes so that you may see. I reprove and discipline those whom I love. Be earnest, therefore, and repent. Listen! I am standing at the door, knocking; if you hear my voice and open the door, I will come in to you and eat with you, and you with me.

REVELATION 3:17–20

Correcting the Sinner

$\mathscr{J}$t is normal and necessary for a mature Christian to have to confront, at some time or other, the inevitable shortcomings of Christians—of others as well as of himself. It is both dishonest and unfaithful for a Christian to imagine that the only way to preserve his faith in the Church is to convince himself that everything is always, in every way, at all times ideal in her life and activity. History is there to prove the contrary. It is unfortunately true that Christians themselves, for one reason or another, may in the name of God himself and of his truth, cling to subtle forms of prejudice, inertia, and mental paralysis. Indeed there may even be serious moral disorders and injustices where holiness should prevail....

The Christian must learn how to face these problems with a sincere and humble concern for truth and for the glory of God's Church. He must learn to help correct these errors, without falling into an indiscreet or rebellious zeal....

LIFE AND HOLINESS

❖ ❖ ❖

God of love, help us to hear your knock on the door to our hearts so that we may not fail to be invited to your eternal banquet. Amplify in us the spirit of courage and love so that we may surrender our tendencies toward moral dysfunction and prideful self-indulgence. Give us the wisdom we need to face the problems of our world, our families, ourselves with radical honesty and appropriate sensitivity. Keep our heads from the sands so we may address the real improprieties we find around us. Let us work to heal at least one wound this Advent. Amen.

When he [Jesus] was sitting on the Mount of Olives, the disciples came to him privately, saying, "Tell us...what will be the sign of your coming and of the end of the age?" Jesus answered them...."But about that day and hour no one knows, neither the angels of heaven, nor the Son, but only the Father. For as the days of Noah were, so will be the coming of the Son of Man. For as in those days before the flood they were eating and drinking, marrying and giving in marriage, until the day Noah entered the ark, and they knew nothing until the flood came and swept them all away, so too will be the coming of the Son of Man. Then two will be in the field; one will be taken and one will be left. Keep awake therefore, for you do not know on what day your Lord is coming."

MATTHEW 24:3–4, 36–42

The Three Advents

*S*aint Bernard frequently returns to the idea of the "three Advents" of Christ. The first of these is the one in which He entered into the world, having received a Human Nature in the womb of the Blessed Virgin Mary. The third is the Advent which will bring Him into the world at the end of time to judge the living and the dead....

We learn to recognize the present Advent that is taking place at every moment in our own earthly life as wayfarers. We awaken to the fact that every moment of time is a moment of judgment, that Christ is passing by and that we are judged by our awareness of His passing. If we join Him and travel with Him to the Kingdom, the judgment becomes for us salvation. But if we neglect Him and let Him go by, our neglect is our condemnation! No wonder Saint Bernard would not have us ignorant of the Second Advent.

SEASONS OF CELEBRATION

✤ ✤ ✤

Sovereign Creator, you who know the signs of the end of the age, sweep away our submersion in the flood of our present daily activities and prepare us for your coming now and at the final judgment. Let us see this "middle Advent" as our time of preparation and awareness of our ultimate goal and ultimate good, eternal life with you in paradise. In this beginning let us see our ending and our new beginning. Amen.

[T]he angel Gabriel was sent by God to a town in Galilee called Nazareth, to a virgin engaged to a man whose name was Joseph, of the house of David. The virgin's name was Mary. And he came to her and said, "Greetings, favored one! The Lord is with you." But she was much perplexed by his words and pondered what sort of greeting this might be. The angel said to her, "Do not be afraid, Mary, for you have found favor with God. And now you will conceive in your womb and bear a son, and you will name him Jesus. He will be great, and will be called the Son of the Most High, and the Lord God will give to him the throne of his ancestor David.

LUKE 1:26–32

A Woman Clothed in Light

*T*he genuine significance of Catholic devotion to Mary is to be seen in the light of the Incarnation itself. The Church cannot separate the Son and the Mother. Because the Church conceives of the Incarnation as God's descent into flesh and into time, and His great gift of Himself to His creatures, she also believes that the one who was closest to Him in this great mystery was the one who participated most perfectly in the gift....

Mary, who was empty of all egotism, free from all sin, was as pure as the glass of a very clean window that has no other function than to admit the light of the sun. If we rejoice in that light, we implicitly praise the cleanness of the window. And of course it might be argued that in such a case we might well forget the window altogether. This is true. And yet the Son of God, in emptying Himself of His majestic power, having become a child, abandoning Himself in complete dependence to the loving care of a human Mother, in a certain sense draws our attention once again to her. The Light has wished to remind us of the window, because He is grateful to her and because He has an infinitely tender and personal love for her.

NEW SEEDS OF CONTEMPLATION

❖ ❖ ❖

Lady Mary, you whose "yes" opened the door to our salvation, show us how we can say "yes" without reservations. Teach us to wait, as we hang in the balance of the past and the possible. Let us make loving choices as you did, acquiescing freely in God's plan for us. Mother us as we make our way to your son. Amen.

DAY 9

The Assyrian came down from
the mountains of the north;
he came with myriads of his warriors....
But the Lord Almighty has foiled them
by the hand of a woman.
For their mighty one did not fall by
the hands of the young men,
nor did the sons of the Titans strike him down,
nor did tall giants set upon him;
but Judith daughter of Merari
with the beauty of her countenance undid him.
For she put away her widow's clothing
to exalt the oppressed in Israel.
She anointed her face with perfume;
she fastened her hair with a tiara
and put on a linen gown to beguile him.

Her sandal ravished his eyes,
her beauty captivated his mind,
and the sword severed his neck!

JUDITH 16:3, 5–9

Mary, the "Royal Way"

God willed that the Blessed Virgin Mary play a central part in the Mystery of the Incarnation and of our Redemption. He willed that the salvation of the world should depend on her consent. Mary is the "royal way" by which the King of Glory descended into the world in order to restore fallen mankind to its destined place in heaven....If we leave her out of the Sacrament of Advent we shall never fully penetrate its mystery, since we need to go forth to meet our Savior on the same Road by which He came to us.

SEASONS OF CELEBRATION

❖ ❖ ❖

O Royal Daughter of David, who causes evil to fall by means of your simple assent to the Holy Spirit, beguile us with your beauty so that we may likewise embrace and trust God's will. Give us the grace to be both prudent and wholehearted in our actions. Give us the faith to wait and wonder without faltering from the road we have undertaken. Amen.

DAY 10

[A] woman in that city, who was a sinner, having learned that he [Jesus] was eating in the Pharisee's house, brought an alabaster jar of ointment. She stood behind him at his feet, weeping, and began to bathe his feet with her tears and to dry them with her hair…. [Jesus] said to Simon, "Do you see this woman? I entered your house; you gave me no water for my feet, but she has bathed my feet with her tears and dried them with her hair. You gave me no kiss, but from the time I came in she has not stopped kissing my feet. You did not anoint my head with oil, but she has anointed my feet with ointment. Therefore, I tell you, her sins, which were many, have been forgiven; hence she has shown great love. But the one to whom little is forgiven, loves little."

LUKE 7:37–38, 44–47

Love and Forgiveness

*P*enance is love which is simple enough and enlightened enough to seek *mercy* and because it seeks mercy, it has already been forgiven. Hence, [the] gospel of Mary Magdalen in the house of Simon the Leper. "Many sins are forgiven her because she has loved much" (Lk 7:47). The first are those who have received mercy and who know that the ways of the Lord are simple because they are the ways of love. Simon and the Pharisees who do not understand love cannot receive the teachings of Jesus about forgiveness, and since they do not feel any need of mercy, the question of forgiveness and love is purely an abstract one....So the truth remains that Jesus is the Way, the Truth, and the Life. In Him the Father has forgiven us and no man comes to the Father but by Him. Penance without the love of Christ is, therefore, wasted. It is useless.

A SEARCH FOR SOLITUDE: THE JOURNALS OF THOMAS MERTON,
VOLUME THREE: 1952–1960

✦ ✦ ✦

Almighty and Forgiving God, oblige us to "make straight the way of the Lord" as did John the Baptist when he announced the coming of the Lord. Help us to greet the presence of the Savior this Advent with the ointment of true repentance, the water of true mercy, and the acceptance of true love, as did Mary Magdalen when she visited the house of Simon. Help us to differentiate between frivolity and genuine fun, lust and love, truth and hollow words. Amen.

DAY 11

But you were angry, and we sinned;
because you hid yourself we transgressed.
We have all become like one who is unclean,
and all our righteous deeds are like a filthy cloth.
We all fade like a leaf, and our iniquities,
like the wind, take us away.
There is no one who calls on your name,
or attempts to take hold of you;
for you have hidden your face from us,
and have delivered us into the of our iniquity.
Yet, O LORD, you are our Father;
we are the clay, and you are our potter;
we are all the work of your hand.

ISAIAH 64:5–8

This Is God's Work

We need to remind ourselves that what we are doing is not a human action; it is divine. This is God's work, not our work. We must be very conscious of that fact because today...people are too often carried away by the merely human side of what is to be done, and they concentrate too much on their own work, their own efforts, and even their own desires, fancies, and inclinations. All these things are good, but they are secondary, and what is secondary has to remain in second place. What is first is God's work, God's Spirit.

THOMAS MERTON IN ALASKA

❖ ❖ ❖

Artist-King, you who created us from impure clay and whose skill is manifest in the things of the world, let us ever acknowledge the wonder of your work. Bring us the keystone, the tent peg, the center of the circle who will repair our lowly house and heart with a firm hand. We wait in weariness for the arrival of one who will leave only the chosen standing. Draw us together as daughters and sons of God. Amen.

DAY 12

I am the vine, you are the branches. Those who abide in me and I in them bear much fruit, because apart from me you can do nothing. Whoever does not abide in me is thrown away like a branch and withers; such branches are gathered, thrown into the fire, and burned. If you abide in me, and my words abide in you, ask for whatever you wish, and it will be done for you. My Father is glorified by this, that you bear much fruit and become my disciples. As the Father has loved me, so I have loved you; abide in my love. If you keep my commandments, you will abide in my love, just as I have kept my Father's commandments and abide in his love. I have said these things to you so that my joy may be in you, and that your joy may be complete.

JOHN 15:5–11

Great Joy

The Nativity message is the message not only of joy but of *the* joy: the GREAT JOY which all the people of the world have always expected without fully realizing what it was. It is the joy of eschatological fulfillment which we seek, in the depths of our hearts, from the moment that we are beings endowed with conscious life....

Now, in the Nativity of Christ, the Great Joy is announced, in which all the ambiguities are swept aside and all men are confronted with the clear possibility of a decision that will not only help them to put together the pieces of lives wrecked in individual failure but will even make sense out of the lives of all men of all time.

LOVE AND LIVING

❖ ❖ ❖

Giver of Peace, inspire all peoples with your meekness and humility of heart. Heal the strife and animosity that separate your sons and daughters and all the nations of the world. You who came to save us, endow us with loving intentions and loving actions. Let the peace of Bethlehem be with us always. Grant us the peace of justice, the peace of charity, and eternal peace with you. Amen.

Now it is evident that no one is justified before God by the law; for "The one who is righteous will live by faith." But the law does not rest on faith; on the contrary, "Whoever does the works of the law will live by them." Christ redeemed us from the curse of the law by becoming a curse for us—for it is written, "Cursed is everyone who hangs on a tree"—in order that in Christ Jesus the blessing of Abraham might come to the Gentiles, so that we might receive the promise of the Spirit through faith.

GALATIANS 3:11–14

Outside the Law

*Y*ou realize that prayer takes us beyond the law. When you are praying you are, in a certain sense, an outlaw. There is no law between the heart and God. The law is outside our intimate relationship with God and if you bring a law into the intimate relationships with God, you mess things up. Between the soul and God there are no laws. But that is not a natural situation; it is the result of redemption, the result of Christ.

THOMAS MERTON IN ALASKA

❖ ❖ ❖

Blessed Jesus, you who loved those outside the law, who sat down to eat with tax collectors, who kept company with sinners, who cured the alien Samaritan, help us go beyond the law into an intimate relationship with you. Transform us from literal-minded legalists into your grace-filled children. Take us by the hand and guide us home. Amen.

DAY 14

They shall come and sing aloud
on the height of Zion,
and they shall be radiant over
the goodness of the LORD,
over the grain, the wine, and the oil,
and over the young of the flock and the herd;
their life shall become like a watered garden,
and they shall never languish again.
Then shall the young women rejoice in the dance,
and the young men and the old shall be merry.
I will turn their mourning into joy,
I will comfort them,
and give them gladness for sorrow.

JEREMIAH 31:12–13

The Gardener of Gethsemani

There was an old Father at Gethsemani....He was absolutely obsessed with gardening, but he had an abbot for a long time who insisted he should do anything but gardening, on principle....Finally when the old abbot died and the new abbot came in, it was tacitly understood that Father Stephen was never going to do anything except gardening, and so...he just gardened from morning to night. He never came to Office, never came to anything, he just dug in his garden. He put his whole life into this and everybody sort of laughed at it....

He didn't have to be unusual that way: that was the way it panned out. This was a development that was frustrated, diverted into a funny little channel, but the real meaning of our life is to develop people who really love God and who radiate love, not in a sense that they feel a great deal of love, but that they simply are people full of love who keep the fires of love burning in the world. For that they have to be...fully themselves—real people.

THOMAS MERTON IN ALASKA

✦ ✦ ✦

Shoot of Jesse, our roots go back to that garden in Eden, to the paradise sold for an apple. The birth of your Son has reopened the gates of heaven and rained down blessings on our parched souls. As we relish the new light of the sun which nurtures our own "gardens" on earth, let us develop into real people who talk not about love but who actually practice the love of God (and through him, love for their neighbors) with a radiant peace. Let us flower in the place you have given us. Amen.

For God alone my soul waits in silence;
from him comes my salvation.
He alone is my rock and my salvation,
my fortress; I shall never be shaken.
How long will you assail a person,
will you batter your victim, all of you,
as you would a leaning wall,
a tottering fence?
Their only plan is to bring down
a person of prominence.
They take pleasure in falsehood;
they bless with their mouths,
but inwardly they curse.
For God alone my soul waits in silence,
for my hope is from him.

PSALM 62:1–5

Tyranny of Noise

*W*e have to realize that sometimes human beings deliberately create noise. People with frustrated wills come together to make noise that causes others to suffer while they themselves do not suffer. This is one way for a frustrated person to "get even." We have to resist this. There is a note of supreme injustice in noisemaking: the noise made by one person can compel another person to listen. This applies to chitchat as well as to industrial noises.

THE SPRINGS OF CONTEMPLATION

✤ ✤ ✤

Gloom-Slayer, come with the refreshing silence of your peace. Stifle the empty clamor of this too-often secularized Christmas season, and set us free to reject the greed and waste so prevalent around us. Let us confirm our convictions without speech, praising you with our actions and our lives as dazzling witnesses to Christ. Amen.

DAY 16

"*Beware of practicing your piety before others in order to be seen by them; for then you have no reward from your Father in heaven.*

"*So whenever you give alms, do not sound a trumpet before you, as the hypocrites do in the synagogues and in the streets, so that they may be praised by others. Truly I tell you, they have received their reward. But when you give alms, do not let your left hand know what your right hand is doing, so that your alms may be done in secret; and your Father who sees in secret will reward you.*"

MATTHEW 6:1–4

Giving Without Strings

*A*n old master went from India to China to see the emperor, who was already a Buddhist. The emperor said to the Zen master: "I have built temples, put up pagodas, and started monasteries. What is my reward?" And the master replied: "You don't get any. There's no reward for you." The emperor was all shook up, thought about it, and after a while realized what was meant. If you need something else as a reward, your *giving* is a fiction.

THE SPRINGS OF CONTEMPLATION

✤ ✤ ✤

Light of the World, shine forth on us and banish our fears and fickleness. As you are a gift freely given, remind us that as your children, our generosity should be untarnished by the expectations of rewards. Let each gift given this season be unadulterated by the need for reciprocity. Keep us from counting—our losses, our gains, our goods, our bads, our costs, our profits. Instead we give you the record book so that you may judge us according to your standards, not our own. Amen.

DAY 17

For a child has been born for us,
a son given to us;
authority rests upon his shoulders;
and he is named
Wonderful Counselor, Mighty God,
Everlasting Father, Prince of Peace.
His authority shall grow continually,
and there shall be endless peace
for the throne of David and his kingdom.
He will establish and uphold it
with justice and with righteousness
from this time onward and forevermore.

ISAIAH 9:6–7

He Is Born to Us

*N*ot only is Jesus born in Bethlehem to save us from sin. Not only do we celebrate Christmas to recall to mind the consoling fact that He is our Redeemer. Not only does He come bringing us graces and gifts. Not only is He born to give Himself in some manner to us. There is much more: He is born in Bethlehem in order that He may be born in us. He gives Himself to us as a child in order to share with us not only His infant smiles and caresses, but above all His very birth and infancy. He is born Son of Man in order that we may be born sons of God, our souls being Bethlehems in which He is born "for us."

THE CHRISTMAS SERMONS OF BL. GUERRIC OF IGNY

✤ ✤ ✤

Good Shepherd of Souls, keep us in the safe company of your guardianship. Sweetly oversee the flock and keep us from the orphanage of sin. Speed our steps on our pilgrimage with you to the cross and, from there, to our hoped-for home in heaven. Amen.

DAY 18

[T]he Lord my God will come, and all the holy ones with him.

On that day there shall not be either cold or frost. And there shall be continuous day (it is known to the Lord), not day and not night, for at evening time there shall be light.

On that day living waters shall flow out from Jerusalem, half of them to the eastern sea and half of them to the western sea....

And the Lord will become king over all the earth; on that day the Lord will be one and his name one....On that day there shall be inscribed on the bells of the horses, "Holy to the Lord."

ZECHARIAH 14:5B–9, 20

The Bells of the Lord

*B*ells are meant to remind us that God alone is good, that we belong to him, that we are not living for this world.

They break in upon our cares in order to remind us that all things pass away and that our preoccupations are not important.

They speak to us of our freedom, which responsibilities and transient cares make us forget.

They are the voice of our alliance with the God of heaven.

They tell us that we are His true temple. They call us to peace with Him within ourselves.

The bells say: business does not matter. Rest in God and rejoice, for this world is only the figure and promise of a world to come, and only those who are detached from transient things can possess the substance of eternal promise.

The bells say: we have spoken for centuries from the towers of the great churches. We have spoken to the saints, your fathers, in their land. We called them, as we call you, to sanctity.

THOUGHTS IN SOLITUDE

❖ ❖ ❖

Eternal Father, let the bells of Christmas signify gentleness as the answer to all violence, tenderness as the answer to the world's harshness, light as the answer to the dark shadows of our misunderstandings, hope as the answer to the meaning of life. Amen.

DAY 19

Long ago God spoke to our ancestors in many and various ways by the prophets, but in these last days he has spoken to us by a Son, whom he appointed heir of all things, through whom he also created the worlds. He is the reflection of God's glory and the exact imprint of God's very being, and he sustains all things by his powerful word.

HEBREWS 1:1–3

Seeds of Sorrow in the Story of Joy

*I*f we...accept God's revelation of Himself in the Infant of Bethlehem, we must realize also that this acceptance has grave consequences for our lives. It means accepting One for whom there is no room in the "inn" of an excited and distraught world....We see this in the disturbing symbol of that census which brings "the whole world" into the books of a Roman imperial power. If we accept this Infant as our God, then we accept our own obligation to grow with Him in a world of arrogant power and travel with Him as He ascends to Jerusalem and to the Cross, which is the denial of power.

LOVE AND LIVING

❖ ❖ ❖

Emmanuel, come. Do not delay. Bring joy to this wretched world and say once more, "Let there be light." This babe in swaddling clothes shines abroad in the whole universe, but contradicts the expectations of his lost children who await his coming. He comes not in royal majesty, nor as a warrior-king making justice victorious. He came instead as a poor child in a manger, attended by the ox and sheep, and watched over by his young mother and stepfather. Even so, we are no longer alone, we are no longer without hope. Amen.

DAY 20

My brothers and sisters, whenever you face tri-
als of any kind, consider it nothing but joy, be-
cause you know that the testing of your faith
produces endurance; and let endurance have is
full effect, so that you may be mature and com-
plete, lacking in nothing.

If any of you is lacking in wisdom, ask God
who gives to all generously and ungrudgingly,
and it will be given you. But ask in faith, never
doubting, for the one who doubts is like a wave
of the sea, driven and tossed by the wind; for
the doubter, being double-minded and unstable
in every way, must not expect to receive any-
thing from the Lord.

JAMES 1:2–8

Advent Optimism

*I*t is important to remember the deep, in some ways an-guished seriousness of Advent, when the mendacious celebrations of our marketing culture so easily harmonize with our tendency to regard Christmas, consciously or otherwise, as a return to our own innocence and our own infancy....

But the Church, in preparing us for the birth of a "great prophet," a Savior and a King of Peace, has more in mind than seasonal cheer. The Advent mystery focuses the light of faith upon the very meaning of life, of history, of man, of the world and of our own being. In Advent we celebrate the coming and indeed the *presence* of Christ in our world.

SEASONS OF CELEBRATION

✦ ✦ ✦

Star of David, make your ways known to us. Teach us your truths, guide us in the paths of righteousness, pardon our sins, erase our guilt, rescue us in the arms of your mercy. Amen.

The LORD dealt with Sarah as he had said, and the LORD did for Sarah as he had promised. Sarah conceived and bore Abraham a son in his old age, at the time of which God had spoken to him. Abraham gave the name Isaac to his son whom Sarah bore him. And Abraham circumcised his son Isaac when he was eight days old, as God had commanded him. Abraham was a hundred years old when his son Isaac was born to him. Now Sarah said, "God has brought laughter for me; everyone who hears will laugh with me." And she said, "Who would ever have said to Abraham that Sarah would nurse children? Yet I have borne him a son in his old age."

GENESIS 21:1–7

Servant of Our Lady

*S*ince the diaconate Our Lady has taken possession of my heart. Maybe, after all, *she* is the big grace of the diaconate. She was given to me with the book of the Gospels which, like her, gives Christ to the world. I wonder what I have been doing all my life not resting in her heart which is the heart of all simplicity. All life, outside of her perfect union with God, is too complicated.

Lady, I am your deacon, your own special and personal deacon. What made me want to laugh in the middle of the Gospel this morning was the fact that you were doing the singing and I was just resting and sailing along.

THE SIGN OF JONAS

✦ ✦ ✦

God of surprises, let us be your Christ-bearer, your servant, your deacon in this world grown too distracting and complicated. Make us ready for the gifts you give, the grace you impart, the opportunities you make available to help us grow in holiness. Grant that our eyes might be open to see, our ears to listen, our hearts to love, and our mouths to laugh with delight and joy when our awareness of your presence informs any moment of the day. Amen.

DAY 22

God, who is rich in mercy, out of the great love with which he loved us even when we were dead through our trespasses, made us alive together with Christ—by grace you have been saved—and raised us up with him and seated us with him in the heavenly places in Christ Jesus, so that in the ages to come he might show the immeasurable riches of his grace in kindness toward us in Christ Jesus. For by grace you have been saved through faith, and this is not your own doing; it is the gift of God—not the result of works, so that no one may boast.

EPHESIANS 2:4–9

Our True Identity

We ourselves have become Someone else. We remain ourselves, fully ourselves. Yet we are aware of a new principle of activity. We are fulfilled by an Identity that does not annihilate our own, which is ours, and yet is "received." It is a Person eternally other than ourselves. This Identity is Christ, God. We discover something of the theological reality that human nature has been, by Him, not absorbed, but *assumed*. He took to Himself a concrete individual nature: but that nature was our nature....

BREAD IN THE WILDERNESS

✣ ✣ ✣

Father of miracles, transform us. Shape our will according to your own. Move to elevate us with your grace, let us come to know the charms of your love that feeds our souls. Let your love open up the windows to our hearts, let your hope blanket us when we despair; may the love that you give us take us home, for apart from you there is no life. Amen.

DAY 23

"Now the parable is this: The seed is the word of God. The ones [seeds] on the path are those who have heard; then the devil comes and takes away the word from their hearts.... The ones [seeds] on the rock are those who, when they hear the word, receive it with joy. But these have no root; they believe only for a while and in a time of testing fall away. As for what fell among the thorns, these [seeds] are the ones who hear; but as they go on their way, they are choked by the cares and riches and pleasures of life, and their fruit does not mature. But as for that in the good soil, these [seeds] are the ones who, when they hear the word, hold it fast in an honest and good heart, and bear fruit with patient endurance."

LUKE 8:11–15

Seeds of True Joy

I believe that, where the Lord sees the small point of poverty, extenuation, helplessness which is the heart of a monk after very long and very dry celebrations in choir, when He sees the point of indigence to which this one is reduced, He Himself cannot refuse to enter this anguish, to take flesh in it so to speak, making it instantly a small seed of infinite joy and peace and solitude in the world. There is for me no sense, no truth in anything that elaborately contrives to hide this precious poverty, this seed of tears which is also the seed of true joy. Demonstrations and distractions that try to take one away from this are futile. They can become infidelities if they are eagerly sought.

CONJECTURES OF A GUILTY BYSTANDER

✦ ✦ ✦

Seed of Wisdom, you have given me the means by which to hear your voice. Through the Scriptures that I read, strengthen me in my weakness, make me firm in my resolve to do your will, according to your Word. May the Scriptures I read during this Advent season help to shape me as you desire. I ask this through your son, our Lord, Jesus Christ. Amen.

DAY 24

But you, O Bethlehem of Ephrathah,
who are one of the little clans of Judah,
from you shall come forth for me
one who is to rule in Israel,
whose origin is from of old,
from ancient days.
Therefore he shall give them up until the time
when she who is in labor has brought forth;
then the rest of his kindred shall return
to the people of Israel.
And he shall stand and feed his flock
in the strength of the LORD,
in the majesty of the name of the LORD his God.

And they shall live secure,
for now he shall be great
to the ends of the earth;
and he shall be the one of peace.

MICAH 5:2–5

A Time of New Beginnings

Liturgically speaking, you could hardly find a better time to become a monk than Advent. You begin a new life, you enter into a new world at the beginning of a new liturgical year. And everything that the Church gives you to sing, every prayer that you say in and with Christ in His Mystical Body is a cry of ardent desire for grace, for help, for the coming of the Messiah, the Redeemer.

The soul of a monk is a Bethlehem where Christ comes to be born—in the sense that Christ is born where His likeness is reformed by grace, and where His Divinity lives, in a special manner, with His Father and His Holy Spirit, by charity, in this "new incarnation," this "other Christ."

THE SEVEN STOREY MOUNTAIN

❖ ❖ ❖

God of growth and love, may the little seed that you have planted in me bear much fruit. May the people I encounter come to know you by the words and actions of my love—a love that I first came to know by your words and actions. Prepare my soul for the coming of the Lord, and continue to have me serve you as an instrument of your love. I ask this through your son, our Lord, Jesus Christ. Amen.

DAY 25

And the Word became flesh and lived among us, and we have seen his glory, the glory as of a father's only son, full of grace and truth....From his fullness we have all received, grace upon grace. The law indeed was given through Moses; grace and truth came through Jesus Christ. No one has ever seen God. It is God the only Son, who is close to the Father's heart, who has made him known.

JOHN 1:14, 16–18

God's Glory

od, without being touched by them, without being mixed in with His creatures, without descending Himself to the level of their joy, shares with them His secret, His innocence, His being, His mystery. That is what we mean by glory. That is what His creatures have to give Him: glory. But what is glory? God's glory is God in them without touching them. God in them without being touched by them. God giving them everything and retaining His own infinite separation. God being their Father without being related to them. They are related to Him, but never come near Him Who is within them. God's glory and God's shyness are one. His glory is to give them everything and to be in the midst of them as unknown.

THE SIGN OF JONAS

✤ ✤ ✤

Word that became flesh, you have reunited mankind with the Divine. Without you we are nothing.

Fulfillment of the Scriptures, you are the new law. Write your law upon our hearts that we may live and love according to your will.

Son of the Father's heart, we are not worthy to receive you—only say the word and we shall be healed. I ask this through your son, our Lord, Jesus Christ. Amen.

DAY 26

Peter said… "Look, we have left everything and followed you. What then will we have?" Jesus said to them, "Truly I tell you, at the renewal of all things, when the Son of Man is seated on the throne of his glory, you who have followed me will also sit on twelve thrones, judging the twelve tribes of Israel. And everyone who has left houses or brothers or sisters or father or mother or children or fields, for my name's sake, will receive a hundredfold, and will inherit eternal life. But many who are first will be last, and the last will be first."

MATTHEW 19:27–30

Vessels of Sunlight

We become like vessels empty of water that they may be filled with wine. We are like glass cleansed of dust and grime to receive the sun and vanish into its light.

Once we begin to find this emptiness, no poverty is poor enough, no emptiness is empty enough, no humility lowers us enough for our desires....

The more our faculties are emptied of their desire and their tension towards created things, and the more they collect themselves into peace and interior silence and reach into the darkness where God is present to their deepest hunger, the more they feel a pure, burning impatience to be free and rid of all the last obstacles and attachments that still stand between them and the emptiness that will be capable of being filled with God.

SEEDS OF CONTEMPLATION

❖ ❖ ❖

Father of the Son who came among us as one of us, you have saved us because of your great love for your creation. Help us keep in mind what is truly important in our lives, that which sustains us. May our eyes and hearts be always set on you. May we receive the sun and vanish into its light. We ask this through our Lord, Jesus Christ. Amen.

DAY 27

For it is the God who said, "Let light shine out
of darkness," who has shone in our hearts to
give the light of the knowledge of the glory of
God in the face of Jesus Christ.

But we have this treasure in clay jars, so
that it may be made clear that this extraordi-
nary power belongs to God and does not come
from us. We are afflicted in every way, but not
crushed; perplexed, but not driven to despair;
persecuted, but not forsaken; struck down, but
not destroyed; always carrying in the body the
death of Jesus, so that the life of Jesus may also
be made visible in our bodies.

2 CORINTHIANS 4:6–10

Crystal Souls, Clay Jars

When a ray of light strikes a crystal, it gives a new quality to the crystal. And when God's infinitely disinterested love plays upon a human soul, the same kind of thing takes place. And that is the life called sanctifying grace.

The soul of man, left to its own natural level, is a potentially lucid crystal left in darkness. It is perfect in its own nature, but it lacks something that it can only receive from outside and above itself. But when the light shines in it, it becomes in a manner transformed into light and seems to lose its nature in the splendor of a higher nature, the nature of the light that is in it.

So the natural goodness of man, his capacity for love which must always be in some sense selfish if it remains in the natural order, becomes transfigured and transformed when the Love of God shines in it. What happens when a man loses himself completely in the Divine Life within him? This perfection is only for those who are called saints—for those rather who *are* the saints and who live in the light of God alone.

The Seven Storey Mountain

✦ ✦ ✦

God of all creation, everything I see around me, everything I hear, taste, feel, and experience—everything that I am—all of this comes from you. I am grateful for all the blessings, challenges, and opportunities you have given me. I ask you for the grace to face the obstacles and successes that I encounter throughout my life. May I see it all through your eyes. I ask this through your son, our Lord, Jesus Christ. Amen.

DAY 28

Blessed be the God and Father of our Lord Jesus Christ, who has blessed us in Christ with every spiritual blessing in the heavenly places, just as he chose us in Christ before the foundation of the world to be holy and blameless before him in love. He destined us for adoption as his children through Jesus Christ, according to the good pleasure of his will, to the praise of his glorious grace that he freely bestowed on us in the Beloved. In him we have redemption through his blood, the forgiveness of our trespasses, according to the riches of his grace that he lavished on us. With all wisdom and insight he has made known to us the mystery of his will…to gather up all things in him, things in heaven and things on earth.

EPHESIANS 1:3–10

Dynamic Mystery

*T*hese "Mysteries" of Christ are not merely called "Mysteries" because they are too deep for us to understand and are therefore proposed to us to be contemplated with silent and adoring faith. They are not just something you think about and look at. The term *mysterium* in Saint Paul has a dynamic sense. It is the fulfillment of a divine plan, springing forth from the eternal wisdom of God, producing its effect in time and, by virtue of this effect, elevating men from the level of time to that of eternity, from the human level to the divine.

BREAD IN THE WILDERNESS

❖ ❖ ❖

God of glory, you have raised us from our pitiable state by the mystery of your Incarnation. We are not worthy of your love yet you give it freely because your faithfulness abides. Grace us with an ever-deepening commitment to love you and follow your will. May we glorify your greatness in everything we do and say. We ask this through your son, our Lord, Jesus Christ. Amen.

PART II

READINGS *for the* TWELVE DAYS *of* CHRISTMAS

Praise the LORD!
Praise, O servants of the LORD;
praise the name of the LORD.
Blessed be the name of the LORD
from this time on and forevermore.
From the rising of the sun to its setting
the name of the LORD is to be praised.
The LORD is high above all nations,
and his glory above the heavens.
Who is like the LORD our God,
who is seated on high, who looks far down
on the heavens and the earth?
He raises the poor from the dust,
and lifts the needy from the ash heap,
to make them sit with princes,
with the princes of his people.

He gives the barren woman a home,
making her the joyous mother of children.
Praise the LORD!

PSALM 113:1–9

Sunrise of Praise

*S*unrise is an event that calls forth solemn music in the very depths of man's nature, as if one's whole being had to attune itself to the cosmos and praise God for the new day, praise Him in the name of all creatures that ever were or ever will be. I look at the rising sun and feel that now upon me falls the responsibility of seeing what all my ancestors have seen, in the Stone Age and even before it, praising God before me. Whether or not they praised Him then, for themselves, they must praise Him now in me. When the sun rises each one of us is summoned by the living and the dead to praise God.

CONJECTURES OF A GUILTY BYSTANDER

❖ ❖ ❖

 God of all joy and giving,
We thank you for your love,
for the joy you bring,
for the sunrise at dawn,
    and the sunset at dusk,
for our Blessed Mother,
    and all the saints in heaven,
for family and friends,
for the food that we share.
Praise to our Lord forever and ever. Amen.

DAY 2

O Lord....
Let your steadfast love become my comfort
according to your promise to your servant.
Let your mercy come to me, that I may live;
for your law is my delight.
Let the arrogant be put to shame,
because they have subverted me with guile;
as for me, I will meditate on your precepts.
Let those who fear you turn to me,
so that they may know your decrees.
May my heart be blameless in your statutes,
so that I may not be put to shame.
My soul languishes for your salvation;
I hope in your word.

PSALM 119:75–81

Freedom to Hope

The one who hopes in God does not *know* that he is predestined to Heaven. But if he perseveres in his hope and continually makes the acts of will inspired by divine grace he will be among the predestined: for that is the object of his hope and "hope confoundeth not" (Romans 5:5). Each act of hope is his own free act, yet it is also a gift of God. And the very essence of hope is freely to expect all the graces necessary for salvation as free gifts from God. The free will that resolves to hope in His gifts recognizes, by that very fact, that its own act of hope is also His gift: and yet it also sees that if it did not will to hope, it would not let itself be moved by Him. Hope is the wedding of two freedoms, human and divine, in the acceptance of a love that is at once a promise and the beginning of fulfillment.

NO MAN IS AN ISLAND

❖ ❖ ❖

God of hope, without you there is only despair, the void. You are the God of promise, of miracles, of possibility. You are the reason we can hope for life eternal, life with you. Your gift is hope, and we ask that you grace us with the desire to hope only in you, for now and forever. We ask this through your son, Christ our Lord. Amen.

DAY 3

[T]hus says the LORD:
Even the captives of the mighty shall be taken,
and the prey of the tyrant be rescued;
for I will contend with those who contend with you,
and I will save your children.
I will make your oppressors eat their own flesh,
and they shall be drunk with
their own blood as with wine.
Then all flesh shall know
that I am the LORD your Savior,
and your Redeemer, the Mighty One of Jacob.

ISAIAH 49:25–26

Harmony of Grace

It is beautiful to see God's grace working in people. The most beautiful thing about it is to see how the desires of the soul, inspired by God, so fit in and harmonize with grace that holy things seem *natural* to the soul, seem to be part of its very self. That is what God wants to create in us—that marvelous spontaneity in which His life becomes perfectly ours and our life His, and it seems inborn in us to act as His children, and to have His light shining out of our eyes.

THE SIGN OF JONAS

❖ ❖ ❖

Lord of salvation, you who opened the doors of heaven to those who had been lost in sin, invest your creation with the knowledge that you alone can give life, life eternal. You became one of us so that we might be saved. We do nothing to earn your love; it is a love you give without conditions. Grant that we may open a space within ourselves where you can reside. We ask this through your son, Christ our Lord. Amen.

DAY 4

Moses said to God, "If I come to the Israelites and say to them, 'The God of your ancestors has sent me to you,' and they ask me, 'What is his name?' what shall I say to them?" God said to Moses, "I AM WHO I AM." He said further, "Thus you shall say to the Israelites, 'I AM has sent me to you.'" God also said to Moses, "Thus you shall say to the Israelites, 'The LORD, the God of your ancestors, the God of Abraham, the God of Isaac, and the God of Jacob, has sent me to you.'"

EXODUS 3:13–15

Alpha and Omega

*R*epentance is at the same time a complete renewal, a discovery, a new life, and a return to the old, to that which is before everything else that is old. But the old and the new meet in the metanoia, the inner change, that is accomplished by the hearing of God's word and the keeping of it. That which is oldest is also newest because it is the beginning. "I am the Beginning, and I speak to you." "I am the Alpha and the Omega, the first and the last, the beginning and the end." The Jews were scandalized at Christ, who spoke as if He were already known to Abraham. "*Thou art not yet forty years old.*" Christ replied: "Before Abraham was made, I *am.*" The new is within the old because it is the perennial beginning of everything, and emerges from the old, transcending it, having no part in it, eternally renewing its own life. The Gospel is handed down from generation to generation *but it must reach each one of us brand new, or not at all.*

CONJECTURES OF A GUILTY BYSTANDER

✢ ✢ ✢

Alpha and Omega, God "who is," Word of life, open up our ears that we might hear your Gospel message, Good News as bright and fulfilling now as it was when you first came among us in the flesh to proclaim it. May your Word move us to greater love toward our neighbor, our enemy, our family, a stranger in need— for in all of these we see your loving face. We ask this through your son, Christ our Lord. Amen.

DAY 5

"Blessed are the poor in spirit,
for theirs is the kingdom of heaven.
"Blessed are those who mourn,
for they will be comforted.
"Blessed are the meek,
for they will inherit the earth.
"Blessed are those who hunger and thirst
for righteousness, for they will be filled.
"Blessed are the merciful, for they will receive mercy.
"Blessed are the pure in heart, for they will see God.
"Blessed are the peacemakers,
for they will be called children of God.
"Blessed are those who are persecuted
for righteousness' sake,
for theirs is the kingdom of heaven."

MATTHEW 5:3–10

The Yoke of Sin

*D*espair is not permitted to the meek, the humble, the afflicted, the ones famished for justice, the merciful, the clean of heart and the peacemakers. All the beatitudes "hope against hope," "bear everything, believe everything, hope for everything, endure everything" (1 Corinthians 13:7). The beatitudes are simply aspects of love. They refuse to despair of the world and abandon it to a supposedly evil fate which it has brought upon itself. Instead, like Christ himself, the Christian takes upon his own shoulders the yoke of the Savior, meek and humble of heart. This yoke is the burden of the world's sin with all its confusions and all its problems. These sins, confusions and problems are our very own. We do not disown them.

PASSION FOR PEACE

❖ ❖ ❖

Creator, Sanctifier, and Redeemer, you who placed the sun and moon in the sky, you who came among us as a poor carpenter, you who bridged the chasm between God and man wrought by sin: we ask that you make us poor in spirit, meek, hungry for righteousness, merciful, and pure in heart. May we seek peace, accept persecution for righteousness' sake, and always live to glorify your name. We ask this through your son, Christ our Lord. Amen.

DAY 6

Trust in the LORD with all your heart,
and do not rely on your own insight.
In all your ways acknowledge him,
and he will make straight your paths.
Do not be wise in your own eyes;
fear the LORD, and turn away from evil.
It will be a healing for your flesh
and a refreshment for your body.
Honor the LORD with your substance
and with the first fruits of all your produce;
then your barns will be filled with plenty,
and your vats will be bursting with wine.

PROVERBS 3:5–10

Hope and Imagination

We are not perfectly free until we live in pure hope. For when our hope is pure, it no longer trusts exclusively in human and visible means, nor rests in any visible end. He who hopes in God trusts God, Whom he never sees, to bring him to the possession of things that are beyond imagination.

NO MAN IS AN ISLAND

❖ ❖ ❖

God of fulfillment, never-failing Lord, we seem to fail you time and again, trusting too much in our own limited, flawed persons, when you are always there, offering to shoulder our burdens. Grant that we may always place our trust in you, that our hope for deeper love, greater peace, and personal fulfillment reside only in you. We ask this through your son, our Lord, Jesus Christ. Amen.

DAY 7

"[T]he kingdom of heaven will be like this. Ten brides-maids took their lamps and went to meet the bridegroom. Five of them were foolish, and five were wise. When the foolish took their lamps, they took no oil with them; but the wise took flasks of oil with their lamps. As the bride-groom was delayed, all of them became drowsy and slept. But at midnight there was a shout, 'Look! Here is the bridegroom! Come out to meet him.' Then all those bridesmaids got up and trimmed their lamps. The fool-ish said to the wise, 'Give us some of your oil, for our lamps are going out.' But the wise replied, 'No! there will not be enough for you and for us; you had better go to the dealers and buy some for yourselves.' And while they went to buy it, the bridegroom came, and those who were ready went with him into the wedding banquet; and the door was shut. Later the other bridesmaids came

*also, saying, 'Lord, lord, open to us.' But he replied, 'Truly
I tell you, I do not know you.' Keep awake therefore, for
you know neither the day nor the hour."*

MATTHEW 25:1–13

Wise and Foolish

$\mathcal{T}$he virgins in the parable are equally divided. Of the ten,
five are wise, five are foolish. One sometimes wonders
whether, in actual fact, the foolish are not far more numerous
than the wise. It is all too easy to go through life with a supine
and slumbering liberty that is like a lamp without oil—a lamp
that does not give light when it is needed.

We most need the light enkindled in our spirit by the Spirit
of God when the cry goes up "the Bridegroom cometh." And He
comes not only at the end of time, at the *Parousia*, but also at
unpredictable moments in our own individual lives—moments
of crisis, when we are providentially summoned to surpass ourselves, and press onward to the fulfillment of our own personal
destiny.

THE NEW MAN

✤ ✤ ✤

Lord and Bridegroom, grant that we be prepared
for your coming, whenever it may be. May we
not be lax in our faith. Grant that we see with eyes of
faith, so that when you approach as a stranger we see you
there and tend to your needs. Our hearts are yours, O
Lord, come to us, come and find your servant awake and
ready to greet you. We ask this through your son, our
Lord, Jesus Christ. Amen.

DAY 8

In that region there were shepherds living in the fields, keeping watch over their flock by night. Then an angel of the Lord stood before them, and the glory of the Lord shone around them, and they were terrified. But the angel said to them, "Do not be afraid; for see—I am bringing you good news of great joy for all the people: to you is born this day in the city of David a Savior, who is the Messiah, the Lord...." And suddenly there was with the angel a multitude of the heavenly host, praising God and saying,

"Glory to God in the highest heaven,
and on earth peace among those whom he favors!"

When the angels had left them and gone into heaven, the shepherds said to one another, "Let us go now to Bethlehem and see this thing that has taken place, which the Lord has made known to us." So they went with haste and found Mary and Joseph, and the child lying in the manger. When they saw this, they made known what had been told them about this child; and all who heard it were amazed at what the shepherds told them.

LUKE 2:8–11, 13–18

Mary's Poverty

*J*t is most fitting to talk about [Mary] as a Queen and to act as if you knew what it meant to say she has a throne above all the angels. But this should not make anyone forget that her highest privilege is her poverty and her greatest glory is that she is most hidden, and the source of all her power is that she is as nothing in the presence of Christ, of God.

It is because she is, of all the saints, the most perfectly poor and the most perfectly hidden, the one who has absolutely nothing whatever that she attempts to possess as her own, that she can most fully communicate to the rest of us the grace of the infinitely selfless God. And we will most truly possess Him when we have emptied ourselves and become poor and hidden as she is, resembling Him by resembling her.

SEEDS OF CONTEMPLATION

❖ ❖ ❖

Father of love, create in our hearts a desire to seek out Jesus in the darker corners of our world. Grace us with the courage to search for your son in those people who are strange to us, who frighten us, who are different to us. We ask this through your son, our Lord, Jesus Christ. Amen.

DAY 9

At that time Jesus said, "I thank you, Father, Lord of heaven and earth, because you have hidden these things from the wise and the intelligent and have revealed them to infants; yes, Father, for such was your gracious will. All things have been handed over to me by my Father; and no one knows the Son except the Father, and no one knows the Father except the Son and anyone to whom the Son chooses to reveal him.

"Come to me, all you that are weary and are carrying heavy burdens, and I will give you rest. Take my yoke upon you, and learn from me; for I am gentle and humble in heart, and you will find rest for your souls. For my yoke is easy, and my burden is light."

MATTHEW 11:25–30

The Fire of Charity

The Christian Life is nothing else but Christ living in us, by His Holy Spirit. It is Christ's love, sharing itself with us in charity. It is Christ in us, loving the Father, by His Spirit. It is Christ uniting us to our brothers by charity in the bond of this same Spirit.

Jesus often expressed His desire to share with us the mystery of His divine life. He said that He came that we might have life, and have it more abundantly (John 10:10). He came to cast that life of charity like fire upon the earth, and He longed to see it enkindled.

THE LIVING BREAD

✣ ✣ ✣

Lord of giving, you never cease to provide. From the Garden of Eden, to the Israelites in the desert, to the birth of Jesus, to this very day, you continue to give great and small gifts to your creation. Grant within me an ever-growing sense of gratitude, dear God, and help me to appreciate that every good thing in my life has its origin in you. I ask this through your son, our Lord, Jesus Christ. Amen.

DAY 10

*There is therefore now no condemnation for those
who are in Christ Jesus. For the law of the Spirit of
life in Christ Jesus has set you free from the law of
sin and of death. For God has done what the law,
weakened by the flesh, could not do: by sending his
own Son in the likeness of sinful flesh, and to deal
with sin, he condemned sin in the flesh, so that the
just requirement of the law might be fulfilled in us,
who walk not according to the flesh but according
to the Spirit. For those who live according to the
flesh set their minds on the things of the flesh, but
those who live according to the Spirit set their minds
on the things of the Spirit. To set the mind on the
flesh is death, but to set the mind on the Spirit is
life and peace. For this reason the mind that is set
on the flesh is hostile to God; it does not submit to*

God's law—indeed it cannot, and those who are in
the flesh cannot please God.

ROMANS 8:1–8

Living Prudently

*I*t is one thing to live *in* the flesh, and quite another to live *according to* the flesh. In the second case, one acquires that "prudence of the flesh which is opposed to God" because it makes the flesh an end in itself. But as long as we are on this earth our vocation demands that we live spiritually while still "in the flesh."

Our whole being, both body and soul, is to be spiritualized and elevated by grace. The Word Who was made flesh and dwelt among us, Who gave us His flesh to be our spiritual food, Who sits at the right hand of God in a body full of divine glory, and Who will one day raise our bodies also from the dead, did not mean us to despise the body or take it lightly when He told us to deny ourselves. We must indeed control the flesh, we must "chastise it and bring it into subjection," but this chastisement is as much for the body's benefit as for the soul's. For the good of the body is not found in the body alone but in the good of the whole person.

NO MAN IS AN ISLAND

✠ ✠ ✠

God of life, you who lived your human life in perfect service to the Father, grant that we not live according to the flesh, but that we subject our flesh to your will, and employ it in service to you and the glory of your name. We ask this through your son, our Lord, Jesus Christ. Amen.

DAY 11

God gave us eternal life, and this life is in his
Son. Whoever has the Son has life; whoever does
not have the Son of God does not have life....

And this is the boldness we have in him, that
if we ask anything according to his will, he hears
us. And if we know that he hears us in whatever we ask, we know that we have obtained
the requests made of him....

We know that those who are born of God
do not sin, but the one who was born of God
protects them, and the evil one does not touch
them. We know that we are God's children, and
that the whole world lies under the power of
the evil one. And we know that the Son of God
has come and has given us understanding so
that we may know him who is true; and we are

in him who is true, in his Son Jesus Christ. He
is the true God and eternal life.

1 JOHN 5:11–12, 14–15, 18–20

Breath of Life

hen God made man, He did more than command him
to exist. Adam, who was to be the son of God and God's
helper in the work of governing the world He had created, was mysteriously formed by God, as the Old Testament so frequently tells us,
as a potter forms a vessel out of clay. "Then the Lord God formed
man out of the dust of the ground and breathed into his nostrils the
breath of life, and man became a living being." [Genesis 2:7.]

The life of Adam, that is to say the "breath" which was to give
actuality and existence and movement to the whole person of
man, had mysteriously proceeded from the intimate depths of
God's own life. Adam was created not merely as a living and mov-
ing animal who obeyed the command and will of God. He was
created as a "son" of God because his life shared something of the
reality of God's own breath or Spirit.

THE NEW MAN

✣ ✣ ✣

Breath of Life, you who knows us better than we
know ourselves, grant that the words we speak
serve to praise your name and express your love for creation. Prevent us from speaking in any way that hurts
another, but rather let our speech be instructive, uplift-
ing, and always in accordance with your will. We ask this
through your son, our Lord, Jesus Christ. Amen.

DAY 12

When the layer of dew lifted, there on the surface of the wilderness was a fine flaky substance, as fine as frost on the ground. When the Israelites saw it, they said to one another, "What is it?" For they did not know what it was. Moses said to them, "It is the bread that the LORD has given you to eat. This is what the LORD has commanded: 'Gather as much of it as each of you needs, an omer to a person according to the number of persons, all providing for those in their own tents.'" The Israelites did so, some gathering more, some less. But when they measured it with an omer, those who gathered much had nothing over, and those who gathered little had no shortage.

EXODUS 16:14–18

"Our ancestors ate the manna in the wilderness; as it is written, 'He gave them bread from heaven to eat.'" Then Jesus said to them, "Very truly, I tell you, it was not Moses who gave you the bread from heaven, but it is my Father who gives you the true bread from heaven. For the bread of God is that which comes down from heaven and gives life to the world."

JOHN 6:31–33

Body of Christ

The Being Who is present is entirely invisible, because Christ in this Sacrament is present only in the manner of a substance. The substance of a thing is its aptitude to be what it is, its aptitude to exist by itself, its power to be itself. It is the substance that answers our question "what is this?" Now in the Sacrament of the Eucharist, precisely, when we ask this question of the consecrated Host, we must listen to the answer of faith, which responds in the words of Christ "This is My Body." The words "My Body" designate the only substantial being which is now present. There no longer remains anything of the substance of bread. We see the accidents of bread, but they contain the substance of the Body of Christ.

THE LIVING BREAD

❖ ❖ ❖

Providential God, you who gives us all that we need and more, we praise you and thank you for nourishing us with the Bread of Life. There is no greater gift that we have received or will receive in all our days upon this earth. This love overwhelms us. Grant that we may cleave to you throughout our remaining days, until that happy day when we join you in eternity. We ask this through your son, our Lord, Jesus Christ. Amen.

PART III

~~~~~~~~~

A FORMAT for EVENING PRAYER

Format for Nightly Prayer and Reading

The purpose of presenting these two optional formats for nightly readings and prayer is to offer a way to use the material in this book as an opportunity for group or individual prayer. Of course, there are other ways in which to use this material, for example, as a vehicle for meditation or as promptings for completing a prayer journal.

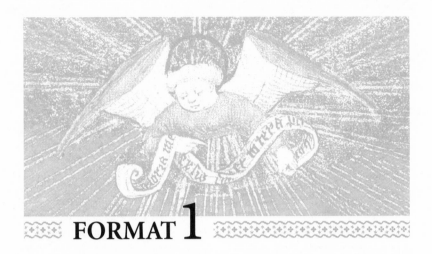

FORMAT 1

OPENING PRAYER

The observance begins with these words:

God, come to my assistance.
Lord, make haste to help me.

followed by:

Glory to the Father and to the Son,
and to the Holy Spirit, as it was in the beginning,
is now, and will be, for ever. Amen. Alleluia!

EXAMINATION OF CONSCIENCE

If this observance is being prayed individually, an examination of conscience may be included. Here is a short examination of conscience; you may, of course, use your own preferred method.

1. Place yourself in a quiet frame of mind.
2. Review your life since your last confession.
3. Reflect on the Ten Commandments and any sins against these commandments.
4. Reflect on the words of the gospel, especially Jesus' commandment to love your neighbor as yourself.
5. Ask yourself these questions: How have I been unkind in thoughts, words, and actions? Am I refusing to forgive anyone? Do I despise any group or person? Am I a prisoner of fear, anxiety, worry, guilt, inferiority, or hatred of myself?

PENITENTIAL RITE (OPTIONAL)

If a group of people are praying in unison, a penitential rite from the Roman Missal may be used:

Presider: Lord Jesus, you came to call all people to yourself: Lord, have mercy.

All: Lord, have mercy.

Presider: Lord Jesus, you come to us in word and prayer: Christ, have mercy.

All: Christ, have mercy.

Presider: Lord Jesus, you will appear in glory with all your saints: Lord, have mercy.

All: Lord, have mercy.

Presider: May almighty God have mercy on us, forgive us our sins, and bring us to life everlasting.

All: Amen.

HYMN: "O COME, O COME, EMMANUEL"

A hymn is now sung or recited. This Advent hymn is a paraphrase of the "Great O" Antiphons written in the twelfth century and translated by John Mason Neale in 1852.

O come, O come, Emmanuel,
And ransom captive Israel;
That mourns in lonely exile here,
Until the Son of God appear.

Refrain: Rejoice! Rejoice!
           O Israel! To thee shall come, Emmanuel!

O come, thou wisdom, from on high,
And order all things far and nigh;
To us the path of knowledge show,
And teach us in her ways to go.

Refrain

O come, O come, thou Lord of might,
Who to thy tribes on Sinai's height
In ancient times did give the law,
In cloud, and majesty, and awe.

Refrain

O come, thou rod of Jesse's stem,
From ev'ry foe deliver them
That trust thy mighty power to save,
And give them vict'ry o'er the grave.

Refrain

O come, thou key of David come,
And open wide our heav'nly home,
Make safe the way that leads on high,
That we no more have cause to sigh.

Refrain

O come, thou Dayspring from on high,
And cheer us by thy drawing nigh;
Disperse the gloomy clouds of night
And death's dark shadow put to flight.

Refrain

O come, Desire of nations, bind
In one the hearts of all mankind;
Bid every strife and quarrel cease
And fill the world with heaven's peace.

Refrain

PSALM 27:7–14—GOD STANDS BY US IN DANGERS

Hear, O LORD, when I cry aloud,
    be gracious to me and answer me!
"Come," my heart says, "seek his face!"
    Your face, LORD, do I seek.
    Do not hide your face from me.

Do not turn your servant away in anger,
    you who have been my help.
Do not cast me off, do not forsake me,
    the LORD will take me up.

Teach me your way, O LORD,
>and lead me on a level path
>because of my enemies.
Do not give me up to the will of my adversaries,
>for false witnesses have risen against me,
>and they are breathing out violence.

I believe that I shall see the goodness of the LORD
>in the land of the living.
Wait for the LORD;
>be strong, and let your heart take courage;
>wait for the LORD!

RESPONSE

I long to see your face, O Lord. You are my light and my help. Do not turn away from me.

SCRIPTURE READING

Read silently or have a presider proclaim the Scripture of the day that is selected.

RESPONSE

Come and set us free, Lord God of power and might. Let your face shine on us and we will be saved.

>*Glory be to the Father, and to the Son,*
>*and to the Holy Spirit, as it was in the beginning,*
>*is now, and will be for ever. Amen.*

SECOND READING

Read the excerpt from Thomas Merton for the day selected.

CANTICLE OF SIMEON

Lord, now you let your servant go in peace;
your word has been fulfilled:
my own eyes have seen the salvation
which you have prepared in the sight of every people:
a light to reveal you to the nations
and the glory of your people Israel.
Glory to the Father, and to the Son, and to the Holy Spirit,
as it was in the beginning, is now, and will be for ever. Amen.

PRAYER

Say the prayer that follows the selected excerpt from Thomas Merton.

BLESSING

May the Lord grant us a restful night and a peaceful death. Amen.

MARIAN ANTIPHON

Loving mother of the Redeemer,
gate of heaven, star of the sea,
assist your people who have fallen yet strive to rise again.
To the wonderment of nature you bore your Creator,
yet remained a virgin after as before.
You who received Gabriel's joyful greeting,
have pity on us poor sinners.

FORMAT 2

OPENING PRAYER

The observance begins with these words:

God, come to my assistance.
Lord, make haste to help me.

followed by:

Glory to the Father and to the Son,
and to the Holy Spirit, as it was in the beginning,
is now, and will be, for ever. Amen. Alleluia!

EXAMINATION OF CONSCIENCE

If this observance is being prayed individually, an examination of conscience may be included. Here is a short examination of conscience; you may, of course, use your own preferred method.

1. Place yourself in a quiet frame of mind.
2. Review your life since your last confession.
3. Reflect on the Ten Commandments and any sins against these commandments.
4. Reflect on the words of the gospel, especially Jesus' commandment to love your neighbor as yourself.
5. Ask yourself these questions: How have I been unkind in thoughts, words, and actions? Am I refusing to forgive anyone? Do I despise any group or person? Am I a prisoner of fear, anxiety, worry, guilt, inferiority, or hatred of myself?

PENITENTIAL RITE (OPTIONAL)

If a group of people are praying in unison, a penitential rite from the Roman Missal may be used:

All: I confess to almighty God,
and to you, my brothers and sisters,
that I have sinned through my own fault
in my thoughts and in my words,
in what I have done,
and in what I have failed to do;
and I ask blessed Mary, ever virgin,
all the angels and saints,
and you, my brothers and sisters,
to pray for me to the Lord our God.

Presider: May almighty God have mercy on us,
forgive us our sins,
and bring us to life everlasting.

All: Amen.

HYMN: "BEHOLD, A ROSE"

A hymn is now sung or recited. This traditional hymn was composed in German in the fifteenth century. It is sung to the melody of the familiar "Lo, A Rose E're Blooming."

Behold, a rose of Judah
From tender branch has sprung,
From Jesse's lineage coming,
As men of old have sung.
It came a flower bright
Amid the cold of winter,
When half spent was the night.

Isaiah has foretold it
In words of promise sure,
And Mary's arms enfolt it,
A virgin meek and pure.
Through God's eternal will
She bore for men a savior
At midnight calm and still.

PSALM 40:1–8—THANKSGIVING FOR DELIVERANCE

I waited patiently for the LORD;
    he inclined to me and heard
       my cry.
He drew me up from the desolate pit,
    out of the miry bog,
and set my feet upon a rock,
    making my steps secure.

He put a new song in my mouth,
  a song of praise to our God.
Many will see and fear,
  and put their trust in the LORD.

Happy are those who make
    the LORD their trust,
  who do not turn to the proud,
    to those who go astray after false
      gods.
You have multiplied, O LORD, my
    God,
  your wondrous deeds and your
    thoughts toward us;
  none can compare with you.
Were I to proclaim and tell of
    them,
  they would be more than can be
    counted.

Sacrifice and offering you do not
    desire,
  but you have given me an open
    ear.
Burnt offering and sin offering
  you have not required.
Then I said, "Here I am;
  in the scroll of the book it is
    written of me.
I delight to do your will, O my God;
  your law is within my heart."

RESPONSE

May all who seek after you be glad in the LORD, may those who find your salvation say with continuous praise "Great is the LORD!"

SCRIPTURE READING

Read silently or have a presider proclaim the Scripture of the day that is selected.

RESPONSE

Lord, you who were made obedient unto death, teach us to always do the Father's will, so that, sanctified by the holy obedience that joins us to your sacrifice, we can count on your immense love in times of sorrow.

> *Glory be to the Father, and to the Son,*
> *and to the Holy Spirit, as it was in the beginning,*
> *is now, and will be for ever. Amen.*

SECOND READING

Read silently or have a presider read the words of Thomas Merton for the day selected.

CANTICLE OF SIMEON

Lord, now you let your servant go in peace;
your word has been fulfilled:
my own eyes have seen the salvation
which you have prepared in the sight of every people:

a light to reveal you to the nations
and the glory of your people Israel.
Glory to the Father, and to the Son,
    and to the Holy Spirit,
as it was in the beginning, is now,
    and will be for ever. Amen.

PRAYER

Recite the prayer that follows the excerpt from Thomas Merton
for the day selected.

BLESSING

Lord, give our bodies restful sleep and let the work we have done
today bear fruit in eternal life. Watch over us as we rest in your
peace. Amen.

MARIAN ANTIPHON

Hail, holy Queen, mother of mercy,
our life, our sweetness, and our hope.
To you do we cry,
poor banished children of Eve.
To you do we send up our sighs,
mourning and weeping in this vale of tears.
Turn then, most gracious advocate,
your eyes of mercy toward us,
and after this exile
show to us the blessed fruit of your womb, Jesus.
O clement, O loving,
O sweet Virgin Mary.

Sources and Acknowledgments

Bread in the Wilderness. New York: New Directions Books, 1953. Copyright © 1953 by Our Lady of Gethsemani Monastery.

The Christmas Sermons of Bl. Guerric of Igny, An Essay by Thomas Merton, Sermons Translated by Sister Rose of Lima, Gethsemani, Kentucky: Abbey of Gethsemani, 1959.

Conjectures of a Guilty Bystander. Garden City, New York: Doubleday & Company, 1965, 1966. Copyright 1965, 1966 by the Abbey of Gethsemani.

Life and Holiness. New York: Herder and Herder, 1963. Copyright © 1963 by the Abbey of Gethsemani.

Excerpts from *The Living Bread* by Thomas Merton. Copyright © 1956 by the Abbey of Our Lady of Gethsemani, Inc. Copyright renewed 1984 by Trustees of the Thomas Merton Legacy Trust. Reprinted by permission of Farrar, Straus, and Giroux, LLC.

Excerpts from *Love and Living* by Thomas Merton. Copyright © 1979 by the Merton Legacy Trust. Reprinted by permission of Farrar, Straus, and Giroux, LLC.

Excerpts from *The New Man* by Thomas Merton. Copyright © 1961 by Thomas Merton. Copyright renewed 1989 by Farrar, Straus & Giroux, Inc. Reprinted by permission of Farrar, Straus, and Giroux, LLC.

No Man Is an Island. New York: Harcourt, Brace and Company, 1955. Copyright © 1955 by the Abbey of Our Lady of Gethsemani.

Passion for Peace: The Social Essays. Edited and with an Introduction by William H. Shannon. New York: Crossroad, 1995. Copyright © 1995 by the Trustees of the Merton Legacy Trust.